Happiness HACKS

HOW TO FIND ENERGY & INSPIRATION

AUBRE ANDRUS

with Karen Bluth, PhD

illustrations by Veronica Collignon

KOHLER ELEMENTARY LIBRARY
KOHLER, WISCONSIN

CAPSTONE PRESS
a capstone imprint

Savvy Books are published by Capstone Press
1710 Roe Crest Drive, North Mankato, Minnesota 56003
www.mycapstone.com

Copyright © 2018 by Capstone Press, a Capstone imprint

All rights reserved. No part of this publication may be reproduced in whole or in part, or stored in a retrieval system, or transmitted in any form or by any means, electronic, mechanical, photocopying, recording, or otherwise, without written permission of the publisher.

The Publisher, Author, and any other content providers of this book are not responsible for any effects that may arise from following the recipes or treatments and using the products from the recipes in this book.

Library of Congress Cataloging-in-Publication Data
is available on the Library of Congress website.

ISBN: 978-1-5157-6820-3 (library hardcover)

Summary: Being happy is good for you. When you're happy, you're energized and motivated to get things done. If you're looking to find more joy in life or are feeling a little defeated, the projects in this book can help. Craft a vision board to help you achieve your goals. Rearrange your room for a change of scenery. Follow a guided 20-minute workout to get your blood pumping. Get motivated by completing a 30-day challenge. Find your way to a happier, healthier you.

Editor: Eliza Leahy
Designer: Tracy McCabe
Art Director: Kay Fraser
Production Specialist: Tori Abraham

Illustrations by Veronica Collignon, except: Shutterstock: Glowonconcept, 36; **Photographs by** Capstone Studio: Karon Dubke, 14 (middle), 15 (all), 22; Shutterstock: 279photo Studio, 12, Aleshyn_Andrei, 44, Antonio Guillem, 20, chuanpis, 29, JeniFoto, 14 (left), lzf, 32, 34, masa44, 14 (top), mavo, 7, mimagephotography, 26, Mivr, 14 (bottom), nito, 14 (right), Olga Rom, 10, Ollyy, 30, Patramansky Oleg, 42, Poprotskiy Alexey, 35, Tuzamka, 6, VGstockstudio, 40
Design Elements by Capstone and Shutterstock
author photo by Ariel Andrus, 48 (top)

Consultant and contributing author: Karen Bluth, PhD
University of North Carolina, Chapel Hill
Chapel Hill, NC

Printed and bound in the United States of America.
010373F17

Table of Contents

How to Use This Book

Cheerful! Energetic! Confident! Motivated! Wouldn't you love to feel that way right now? With this book, you can. Really. Because even when you're feeling the exact opposite — stressed out, frustrated, or overwhelmed — there are tips and tricks that can totally transform your mindset and your emotions.

When you're having a rough day, doing something — anything — can make you feel better. It can be hard to get off the couch on one of those days. But it's amazing what can happen after you take that first step.

The following pages are filled with activities, exercises, advice, prompts, crafts, playlists, and recipes that can help you get there. Flip through the pages and choose the project that speaks to you most in this moment. If that exercise doesn't do the trick, try something else!

However, you can't use this book to solve serious mental health problems such as anxiety disorders, depression, or eating disorders. If at any point you think you need more help than this book can offer, please turn to page 44.

IF YOU'RE FEELING STUCK → TRY A 30-DAY CHALLENGE ON PAGE 10.

IF YOU'RE OFTEN TIRED DURING THE DAY → TRY THE POWER-UP SNACKS ON PAGE 12.

IF YOU'RE UNSURE OF YOUR FUTURE → LEARN HOW TO MAKE A VISION BOARD ON PAGE 22.

IF YOU'RE AFRAID TO STAND OUT → LEARN HOW TO IMPROVE YOUR POSTURE ON PAGE 24.

IF YOU'RE FEELING BORED → TRY REARRANGING YOUR ROOM WITH THE ADVICE ON PAGE 36.

Exude Confidence

Even when your mouth is closed, your body is speaking through your facial expressions, shoulders, eyes, leg placement, hand gestures, and more. First impressions are often made based on body language. If your shoulders are slumped, your arms crossed, and your eyes cast downward, you may not look very approachable. But if you send out more positive signals to the world, you may be more likely to receive them. Positivity attracts positivity, and good body language makes you look friendly, confident, and trustworthy.

For good posture tips, turn to page 24.

6

1. KEEP YOUR HEAD UP.

If you catch someone's gaze, it will make it easier to say hi, share a smile, or ask a question. If you're looking down, you can't do that! Make eye contact when you talk — and when you listen. It shows that you are enjoying the conversation.

2. RELAX YOUR SHOULDERS AND ARMS.

When you're tense, your shoulders shrug up to your ears. And when your arms are crossed, it can give people the impression that you are distant or defensive. Take a deep breath, then relax your shoulders and arms as you breathe out. Wiggle them a little bit to loosen up. Let your arms fall naturally at your sides.

3. MOVE SLOWLY.

Try not to fidget, tap your feet, touch your face, or flail your hands. You'll look nervous! It's OK to use hand gestures when you talk, but try not to overdo it. Move confidently, calmly, and deliberately.

4. SMILE AND NOD.

To show you're listening and interested in a conversation, smile and nod — or laugh when it's appropriate. A smile gives a vote of confidence to someone else. It will make him or her feel more comfortable around you.

Choose Joy

You never know when you'll need a boost. This jar is filled with positivity and can be a daily reminder as to why your life is great.

MY JOY jar

START THE DAY WITH A SMILE!

paper, cut into strips
a marker or pen
a glass jar
stickers, ribbon, and tape

Directions:

On the strips of paper, write down:

YOUR HAPPIEST MEMORIES

QUOTES THAT INSPIRE YOU

YOUR FAVORITE PLACES

NICE THINGS PEOPLE HAVE SAID ABOUT YOU

QUOTES FROM YOUR FAVORITE BOOKS OR MOVIES

AMAZING THINGS YOU'VE ACCOMPLISHED

RANDOM THINGS THAT MAKE YOU SMILE

INSIDE JOKES THAT MAKE YOU LAUGH

SONG LYRICS THAT SPEAK TO YOU

Fold the paper slips and place them inside the jar. Decorate the outside of the jar with stickers, colorful ribbon, or washi tape.

When you're feeling down, grab a strip of paper and keep it with you throughout the day as a reminder. Whenever something makes you happy, write it down and add it to the jar!

Mindfulness Tip: Notice how you feel when you read one of the strips of paper. Those memories are with you always!

"ONLY IN THE DARKNESS CAN YOU SEE THE STARS."
– MARTIN LUTHER KING JR.

30-Day Challenge

Declaring a goal is the easy part. Figuring out how to get there — and sticking to it — takes some serious skill. After all, lots of people are great at making to-do lists, but not everyone is great at getting them done. That's the goal of this challenge.

Get things done!

S	M	T	W	T	F	S
					1	2
3	4	5	6	7	8	9
10	11	12	13	14	15	16
17	18	19	20	21	22	23
24	25	26	27	28	29	30

For the next 30 days, you'll tackle a small goal one day at a time. By the end of month, your goal will be achieved! What's one small goal you'd love to reach? Write it down. Then follow these steps:

1. BREAK THE GOAL INTO SMALL STEPS. ASK YOURSELF, WHAT DO I NEED TO DO TO REACH MY GOAL OVER THE NEXT FOUR WEEKS? FOR EXAMPLE, IF YOUR GOAL IS TO WRITE A SHORT STORY, YOU COULD TURN IT INTO A FOUR-STEP PROCESS: BRAINSTORM AN IDEA, MAKE AN OUTLINE, WRITE THE FIRST DRAFT, AND REVISE THE FINAL DRAFT.

2. SET DEADLINES FOR EACH STEP OVER THE NEXT 30 DAYS. STAY FOCUSED AND STICK TO THEM!

3. TRACK YOUR PROGRESS. WRITE YOUR DEADLINES IN A TO-DO LIST FORMAT AND CROSS OFF EACH ONE THAT YOU MEET.

If you aren't sure where to begin, check out these ideas for your 30-day challenge:

- READ ONE BOOK PER WEEK
- LEARN HOW TO PLAY A SONG ON THE GUITAR OR PIANO
- WRITE A SHORT STORY
- DO A RANDOM ACT OF KINDNESS 30 DAYS IN A ROW
- REORGANIZE AND REDECORATE YOUR BEDROOM
- EXERCISE THREE DAYS A WEEK FOR THE NEXT MONTH
- BRING A LUNCH TO SCHOOL EVERY DAY FOR THE NEXT MONTH
- WORK YOUR WAY UP TO A 5K RUN

When you share your goals with others, they feel more real. And you're more likely to stick to them if you know someone else is watching.

"ANYTHING'S POSSIBLE IF YOU'VE GOT ENOUGH NERVE."
– J.K. ROWLING

Power-Up Afternoon Snacks

You are what you eat! So when you need an afternoon pick-me-up, what else would you grab but an energizing snack? The following recipes include ingredients that naturally provide a boost to your body and your mind. Keep a snack in your bag or locker for emergencies, or pre-make some snacks that are easy to grab at home.

Avocado Toast

YOU WILL NEED:

one slice of toast
half an avocado
olive oil
salt
lemon juice

Avocado is filled with stress-relieving B vitamins. Plus it's delicious!

Directions:

Toast a slice of bread. Slice or mash half an avocado and spread it on the toast with a butter knife. Drizzle with olive oil, then sprinkle with salt and a little lemon juice.

Mindfulness Tip: As you bite into the toast, notice the crispiness of the toast, the smoothness of the avocado, and the tartness of the lemon juice. As you chew, pay attention to what happens to these different textures and tastes as they mix together in your mouth.

YOU WILL NEED:

1 whole-wheat tortilla
hummus
2 slices of turkey deli meat
1 stick of mozzarella string
  cheese

Protein Pinwheels

Your body needs protein to build and repair bones, muscles, and more. Turkey and mozzarella cheese are packed with protein. Whole wheat gives you fiber, which helps you feel full.

Directions:

Spread a thin layer of hummus on one side of the tortilla. Layer turkey slices on top. Place the string cheese at one edge and roll the turkey and tortilla around it. Slice the roll of the tortilla with a knife to create pinwheels.

Triple Threat Trail Mix

YOU WILL NEED:

1 cup (30 g) toasted Os cereal
½ cup (70 g) almonds
½ cup (65 g) dried cherries
¼ cup (45 g) dark chocolate chips
¼ tsp (650 mg) cinnamon

The combination of nuts, cinnamon, and dark chocolate is a powerful mix that may give a boost to your energy and your mood. Cherries add a bit of sweetness and some vitamin C that can help keep you strong.

Directions:

Add ingredients to a bowl and stir. Scoop half-cup servings into resealable plastic bags. Makes about four servings.

YOU WILL NEED:

1 banana
1 cup (215 g) ice cubes
½ cup (80 g) oats
½ cup (130 g) vanilla yogurt
½ cup (118 mL) milk
2 tsp (10 mL) honey
dash of cinnamon (optional)

Power-Up Smoothie

This smoothie is a great energy boost. It's full of fiber, which will keep you feeling full and balanced, so your energy doesn't crash hard later on.

Directions:

Mix all ingredients in a blender until smooth. Makes one smoothie.

"TELL ME WHAT YOU EAT, AND I WILL TELL YOU WHO YOU ARE." – JEAN ANTHELME BRILLAT-SAVARIN

Try Something New

When you take on a challenge, be it a crossword puzzle or an intermediate climbing wall, you build confidence. Overcoming challenges can also help you build your self-esteem. Someone with high self-esteem knows they might fail at something — and they're OK with it. On the next page, you'll find some ways to challenge yourself.

- SAY HI TO A STRANGER.

- TACKLE A HUGE JIGSAW PUZZLE.

- ASK A FRIEND TO TEACH YOU HIS OR HER FAVORITE SPORT.

- MAKE A NEW RECIPE.

- LEARN FIVE PHRASES IN A NEW LANGUAGE.

- DO AS MANY PUSH-UPS AS YOU CAN.

- ONLY SAY POSITIVE THINGS FOR THE REST OF THE DAY. (NO COMPLAINTS!)

- MAKE EYE CONTACT WITH A STRANGER.

- PERFORM A POEM OR SONG IN FRONT OF A GROUP.

- TAKE A COLD SHOWER.

- FINISH A SUDOKU PUZZLE.

- TEACH YOURSELF TO PLAY A SONG ON THE PIANO.

- RAISE YOUR HAND WHEN SOMEONE ASKS FOR A VOLUNTEER.

- START UP A CONVERSATION WITH A STRANGER.

- TAKE THE STAIRS INSTEAD OF THE ESCALATOR.

- CALL UP AN OLD FRIEND JUST TO SAY HI.

- GIVE SOMEONE A COMPLIMENT.

- EAT SOMETHING YOU'VE NEVER TRIED BEFORE.

- DON'T SPEND ANY MONEY FOR AN ENTIRE DAY.

- ASK YOUR FRIENDS TO WRITE DOWN YOUR BEST QUALITIES.

DO SOMETHING YOU WERE ALWAYS AFRAID TO DO.

That's right. It's time to face a fear. Public speaking? Heights? Asking a new friend to hang out? With a little bit of preparation and practice, you can do anything.

TRY SOMETHING YOU'VE FAILED AT BEFORE.

Is there something you've never been good at? Maybe it's drawing a face, baking cookies, or doing a cartwheel. Give it a second shot. Learn from your past mistakes - how can you improve them this time around?

MAKE YOURSELF VULNERABLE.

Sign up for an improvisation class, submit your poetry to a magazine, or audition for the school talent show. Whether it's a chance to embarrass yourself, bare your soul, or get some unwanted attention, the fear and excitement that comes with vulnerability can make you feel alive!

Stretch

Stretching can provide an instant release of built-up tension. Try one of these stretches for a quick but invigorating exercise.

JAW STRETCH

Hold a thumb to your chin and apply pressure to create a slight resistance. Open and close your jaw 10 times.

NECK ROLL

Tilt your chin to your chest. Roll your left ear to your left shoulder. Roll back to the center. Roll your right ear to your right shoulder. Return to center. Repeat 10 times.

NECK STRETCH

Tilt your left ear to your left shoulder as your right arm relaxes at your side. Reach your left hand over your head and let your fingers rest on your right temple. Apply a little bit of pressure as you stretch. Repeat on the right side.

SHOULDER ROTATION

Stand with your back against a wall. Bend your arms at the elbow to make 90-degree angles, and hold your elbows against the wall. Slowly rotate your left arm downward (so your palm touches the wall) and your right arm upward (so the back of your hand touches the wall), then alternate. Repeat 10 times.

SHOULDER STRETCH

This stretch begins on the ground with your knees directly under your hips and your wrists directly underneath your shoulders. Lift your left arm and slide it through the space between your right arm and leg. It should be touching the floor. Rotate your upper body until you feel the stretch. Hold for 10 seconds. Repeat on the other side.

CHEST STRETCH

Lie on your right side with your legs bent at a 90-degree angle. Reach your arms out in front of you so they are perpendicular to your body. Reach your left arm up and over, creating an arch movement, until the arm reaches the ground on the opposite side. Let your gaze follow. Stretch for about 10 seconds. Repeat on the other side.

ARM CIRCLES

Stand with a straight arm extended directly in front of you. Make five slow circles backward. Make five slow circles forward. Repeat on the other side.

If any of these stretches cause pain, stop! Always listen to your body.

"A PERSON WHO NEVER MADE A MISTAKE NEVER TRIED ANYTHING NEW." – ALBERT EINSTEIN

Get Some Sun

Getting some sunshine can give you a quick burst of happiness. Just 15 minutes a day can make a difference.

Over the last couple decades, the sun has gotten a bad rap due to the prevalence of skin cancer. But the truth is that we need a little bit of sun every day — with the protection of sunscreen, of course. There are many reasons why sunshine is good for you. Here are a few:

- SUNLIGHT HELPS YOUR BODY PRODUCE VITAMIN D, WHICH KEEPS YOUR BONES HEALTHY AND STRONG.

- THE SUN HELPS REGULATE YOUR BIOLOGICAL CLOCK. SUNSHINE SIGNALS TO YOUR BODY THAT IT'S DAYTIME, AND DARKNESS SIGNALS THAT IT'S NIGHTTIME.

- SOME PEOPLE GET THE WINTER BLUES, BUT SUNSHINE CAN HELP FIGHT OFF SEASONAL DEPRESSION. IN SHORT, SUNLIGHT MAKES YOU HAPPY!

You don't have to drastically change your routine to incorporate more sunshine into your day. Here are some easy habits you can start that will give your body the vitamin D it needs. Even if you live in an area that gets cold during the winter, you can still do many of these activities year-round. You'll just have to layer appropriately. Don't forget a hat!

INSTEAD OF READING INSIDE . . . MOVE OUTDOORS TO A PARK BENCH.

INSTEAD OF TAKING THE BUS TO SCHOOL . . . RIDE YOUR BIKE.

INSTEAD OF DOING HOMEWORK AT YOUR DESK . . . DO IT OUTSIDE.

INSTEAD OF LISTENING TO MUSIC IN YOUR ROOM . . . LISTEN TO IT WHILE YOU GO FOR A WALK.

INSTEAD OF TAKING A NAP ON THE COUCH . . . NAP ON A BLANKET IN THE GRASS.

INSTEAD OF RUNNING ON A TREADMILL . . . GO FOR A RUN THROUGH YOUR NEIGHBORHOOD.

INSTEAD OF WATCHING TV . . . WATCH A SUNSET.

INSTEAD OF EATING LUNCH INSIDE . . . FIND A PICNIC TABLE UNDER THE SUN.

INSTEAD OF LETTING YOUR DOG OUT IN THE BACKYARD . . . TAKE HIM FOR A WALK.

"A JOURNEY OF A THOUSAND MILES BEGINS WITH A SINGLE STEP." – LAO TZU

Have a Vision

Vision boards, or dream boards, can be hung in your room and can inspire you on a daily basis to keep working toward your goals. Think of each image as a seed that you're planting. One day it will grow into the dream you want to achieve. An everyday reminder encourages you to take action and "water" the seeds you've planted.

Make a Vision Board

What should you put on a vision board? Anything you'd like! Motivational quotes or sayings, words that are important to you, photos that make you happy, people that inspire you, mementos from your favorite places, the goals you want to reach . . . the list goes on and on!

YOU WILL NEED:
images
scissors
glue
shadow box, corkboard,
or poster board

Directions:

1. Gather the materials you'd like to showcase on your vision board. It's best if you can find images that express your goals, emotions, and dreams as opposed to just words. Print designs or photos off of the Internet, cut out images or words from magazines, write out your favorite quotes or sayings, or include photos and mementos of your own.

2. Now glue the items to your board. Let the vision board dry overnight.

3. Display it on your desk, a nightstand, or another place that you'll see every day. Spend five minutes every day (in the morning or at night) getting inspired by your board.

"CREATE THE HIGHEST, GRANDEST VISION POSSIBLE FOR YOUR LIFE, BECAUSE YOU BECOME WHAT YOU BELIEVE." – OPRAH WINFREY

Practice Good Posture

Body language is important — and the way you sit and stand is one of the loudest ways your body speaks to others. Standing proud makes you look more confident and feel more confident too. According to some studies, good posture can put you in a good mood. So enough with the slouching!

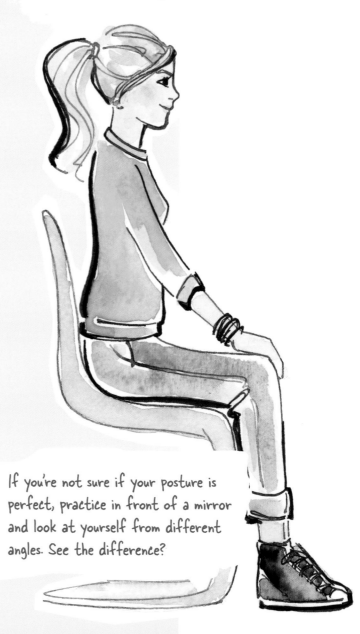

If you're not sure if your posture is perfect, practice in front of a mirror and look at yourself from different angles. See the difference?

Good Standing Posture

PULL YOUR SHOULDERS BACK AND SLIGHTLY PUFF OUT YOUR CHEST.

YOUR STOMACH SHOULD BE PULLED SLIGHTLY INWARD.

KEEP YOUR HEAD LEVEL AND YOUR EARS IN LINE WITH YOUR SHOULDERS.

YOUR FEET SHOULD BE SHOULDER-WIDTH APART.

MAKE SURE YOUR KNEES ARE "SOFT," NOT LOCKED.

PLACE MOST OF YOUR WEIGHT ON THE BALLS OF YOUR FEET.

Good Sitting Posture

YOUR FEET SHOULD REST FLAT ON THE FLOOR AND YOUR THIGHS SHOULD BE PARALLEL TO THE GROUND. IF THEY'RE NOT, FIND A SEAT THAT'S TALLER OR SHORTER.

PRETEND A STRING IS ATTACHED TO THE CENTER OF YOUR HEAD AND IS BEING PULLED UP.

KEEP YOUR HEAD LEVEL AND YOUR EARS IN LINE WITH YOUR SHOULDERS.

RELAX YOUR SHOULDERS. DON'T LET THEM SCRUNCH UP TO YOUR EARS.

Mindfulness Tip: Notice how you feel as you stand up straight. Do you feel a bit better about yourself? And then notice how you feel when you slouch. What changes?

Another easy way to display confidence is to make and keep eye contact. Try it! You'll get better with practice.

"OPTIMISM IS THE FAITH THAT LEADS TO ACHIEVEMENT. NOTHING CAN BE DONE WITHOUT HOPE AND CONFIDENCE." – HELEN KELLER

Loving-Kindness Meditation

Loving-kindness simply means a feeling of friendliness, openheartedness, or warmth. People have been practicing this meditation for thousands of years in places such as India and Southeast Asia. On the following page is a slight variation from the traditional practice.

Mindfulness Tip: It's OK to adjust the phrases if they don't work for you. For example, some people aren't comfortable with "may you." If that's you, feel free to drop that part of the phrase. Others feel more comfortable saying "May you be at peace" rather than "May you feel safe." Find the words that work for you!

Get into a relaxed position, either sitting or lying down.

Make sure you're in a comfortable position where you won't be disturbed for about 15 or 20 minutes.

Think of someone who makes you smile. This can be anyone – a friend, a little kid you know, even your cat or dog. It can be anyone who makes you smile when you think of him or her.

Of course this living being, like all living beings, wants to be happy. Silently and very slowly, repeat some phrases for this living being – thinking about the meaning of the words as you silently say them. Over several minutes, you are taking your time to repeat these phrases.

- "MAY YOU BE HAPPY."
- "MAY YOU FEEL LOVED AND ACCEPTED FOR WHO YOU ARE."
- "MAY YOU FEEL SAFE."

Repeat these phrases until you feel like you have a little bit of a sense of the wish for happiness, love, and safety of this other being.

After repeating these phrases for several minutes, begin letting go of the image of the being who makes you smile. You are bringing to mind an image of yourself as you are sitting or lying here. Now you are repeating silently these same phrases for yourself, taking several minutes to do this.

- "MAY I BE HAPPY."
- "MAY I FEEL LOVED AND ACCEPTED FOR WHO I AM."
- "MAY I FEEL SAFE."

After several minutes, you are letting go of the image of yourself and bringing to mind a "neutral" person. This is someone who you don't have any feelings for one way or the other. It might be someone in one of your classes who you've never thought much about. You are getting a clear image of this person in your mind, and repeating the phrases for them. Remembering to feel the meaning of the words, you are taking your time and doing this slowly.

- "MAY YOU BE HAPPY."
- "MAY YOU FEEL LOVED AND ACCEPTED FOR WHO YOU ARE."
- "MAY YOU FEEL SAFE."

After silently repeating these phrases for several minutes, you are letting go of the image of the neutral person and bringing to mind a "difficult" person. This is someone who annoys you or bothers you in some way. It's best not to choose the most difficult person in your life (at least to start!) but someone who just kind of bugs you. Being a human being, this person also wants to be happy, like all human beings. So now you are taking a few minutes to repeat the phrases silently for this person.

- "MAY YOU BE HAPPY."
- "MAY YOU FEEL LOVED AND ACCEPTED FOR WHO YOU ARE."
- "MAY YOU FEEL SAFE."

Check in with yourself about how you feel about any of these people now. Any different?

Take a Staycation

A short break can do a lot for your peace of mind. Just like you recharge your phone, sometimes you need to recharge your mind and body. Your "staycation" can be done alone or with others — whichever seems more relaxing to you. Look at the itineraries here to get you started, but feel free to tailor them however you'd like.

ITINERARY 1: EDUCATIONAL EXCURSION

Start your day at a museum or zoo that's inspiring to you. If there is a temporary exhibit, workshop, or presentation that especially piques your interest, take advantage of it! Be sure to schedule a few hours to explore, so you don't feel rushed. Go alone or with a friend who is willing to stroll with you at a leisurely pace.

As you walk through the exhibits, take the time to really read everything and learn something new. Bring along a journal so you can take notes or sketch the most inspiring things you see or learn. Don't be afraid to find a seat in your favorite exhibit and stay awhile. Afterward, head to the library where you can check out a book on something that you'd love to learn more about.

ITINERARY 2: CALMING GETAWAY

Take some time to research nearby arboretums, observatories, nature reserves, and trails. You may be surprised at the beauty that's hiding in your own town. Choose the place that looks most serene to you. Someplace with a view of a lake, ocean, mountain, meadow, or river is a good option.

Plan for a long bike ride, hike, or walk on a sunny morning. Take a small blanket, a book, sunscreen, some snacks, and water in a backpack. When you find the perfect spot, stop and read for an hour or two. Or, if you feel inspired, write or draw in a notebook.

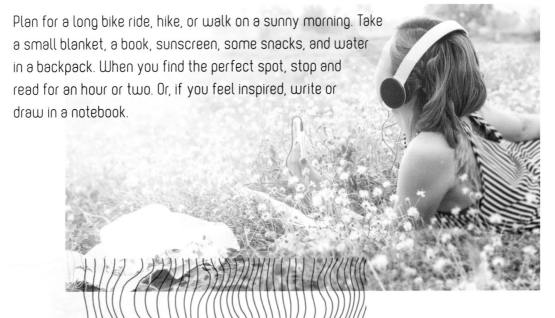

ITINERARY 3: WINDOW SHOPPING

Visit your favorite mall or shopping area with one goal — don't spend any money! Instead, have fun browsing. This is a fun activity to do with friends or family. Get inspired by what you see — a great outfit idea, a bedroom decorating tip, a cool poster, or even an interesting person you encounter.

Feel free to touch, try on, or take pictures of your favorite things. But no buying! If you want to make a game of it, create a scavenger hunt or a photo challenge and set a time limit. Or you can window shop for fantastical things, such as furnishings for your dream home, a gown for a royal ball, or what you might need for a trip around the world.

ITINERARY 4: VIRTUAL VACATION

What's one place you'd love to visit in the world? The Taj Mahal? The Great Wall of China? The Eiffel Tower? Machu Picchu? The Grand Canyon? Angkor Wat? Head to the library and check out a bunch of books on that location. Travel books are an obvious choice, but don't forget about historical biographies and novels that can provide backstory on your dream destination. A librarian can help you gather the best materials.

If you're interested in traveling abroad to a non-English-speaking country, you could check out a language book or CD or download a free language-learning app such as Duolingo. Look in the cookbook section to explore the local cuisine. Then browse the CDs to find some local music. There may even be a DVD for a travel show episode that features your location of choice. If you're really inspired, you could throw a mini party that re-creates your dream destination!

"NOT ALL WHO WANDER ARE LOST." – J.R.R. TOLKIEN

Break a Sweat

Exercise has been proven to make you happy. And it can make you feel more confident, help you fall asleep at night, and suppress anxiety. The list goes on and on! It almost sounds too good to be true. But the reality is that after a workout, you'll be more productive and you'll probably have a more positive outlook. On the following pages is a 20-minute routine you can do in the comfort of your own home.

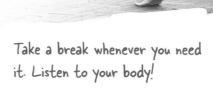

Take a break whenever you need it. Listen to your body!

WHEN DOING CORE EXERCISES, SUCH AS THE ALTERNATING REACH, ELBOW PLANK, AND SIDE PLANK, MAKE SURE TO KEEP YOUR ABDOMINAL MUSCLES TIGHTENED THROUGHOUT. THIS WILL HELP PROTECT YOUR BACK FROM ANY STRAIN.

YOU WILL NEED:

a jump rope
a yoga mat
a stopwatch or clock

MINUTES 0:00–4:00: JUMP ROPE

Jumping is a great full-body workout that gets your heart pumping. To make sure the jump rope is the correct length, place one foot on the center of the rope. Pull the handles up. They should reach your armpits. The best place to jump rope is on a hard surface.

- Single jump with your feet together for 30 seconds.

- For the next 30 seconds, alternate jumping a few inches forward then a few inches backward.

- Rest for 30 seconds. Walk around and grab a small sip of water if you need it. Don't sit.

- Single jump with one foot at a time (like you're running in place) for 30 seconds.

- For the next 30 seconds, alternate jumping a few inches to the left, then a few inches to the right with your legs together.

- Rest for 30 seconds. Walk around and grab a small sip of water if you need it. Don't sit.

- Single jump with one foot at a time (like you're running in place) for 30 seconds.

- For the last 30 seconds, alternate jumping with your feet together and your feet apart (like a jumping jack) for 30 seconds.

MINUTE 4:00–5:00: ALTERNATING REACH

Get on all fours with your wrists directly underneath your shoulders and your knees directly underneath your hips. Now slowly raise and straighten the left arm and the right leg. Repeat with right arm and left leg. Alternate for the next minute.

MINUTE 5:00–6:00: ELBOW PLANK

With your elbows directly underneath your shoulders, get into a push-up position but keep your forearms on the ground. Hold for one minute or as long as you can without your knees touching the ground.

MINUTE 6:00–7:00: SIDE PLANK

From the plank position, twist your body to the left as you raise your left arm straight up. Hold for 30 seconds. Repeat on right side.

KOHLER ELEMENTARY LIBRARY
KOHLER, WISCONSIN

MINUTES 7:00–11:00: JUMP ROPE

Repeat the routine from the previous page.

MINUTE 11:00–11:30: SCISSOR KICKS

Lie on your back. Keep your lower back on the ground throughout, and tighten your abs. Slowly lift your left leg. Now slowly lower your left leg while slowly raising your right leg. Keep your legs as straight as possible and try to keep your heels off the floor. Repeat for 30 seconds.

MINUTE 11:30–12:00: SITTING TWISTS

Sit up with your legs straight in front you. Lean slightly backward with a straight back and lift and bend your knees so you're balancing on your bottom. Clasp your hands together. Twist your upper body and tap the floor on your left side. Repeat on the right. Alternate. Do as many as you can in 30 seconds.

MINUTE 12:00–12:30: SQUAT JUMPS

With your legs a little wider than your shoulders and your toes pointing slightly outward, sit back into a squat position. As you rise back up, jump and straighten your legs. Land lightly on your feet in a squat position. Repeat. Do as many as you can in 30 seconds.

MINUTE 12:30–13:00: WALKING LUNGES

Stand with your feet together and hands on your hips. Step forward with your right leg into a lunge position. Bring your feet back together by moving your left leg to your right. Now repeat on the left side. Alternate for 30 seconds.

MINUTES 13:00–15:00: REPEAT

Repeat the series of four exercises from minutes 11:00 to 13:00.

MINUTES 15:00–19:00: JUMP ROPE

Repeat the first three minutes of the routine on page 33, then march lightly in place for a minute.

MINUTE 19:00–19:30: COBRA POSE

Lie on your stomach as if you're ready to begin a push-up. Now slowly raise only your upper body. Your thighs and feet remain flat on the ground. You should feel the stretch in your stomach and back. Make sure your arms are straight and your shoulders are relaxed.

MINUTE 19:30–20:00: DOWNWARD-FACING DOG

From Cobra position, lower your upper body back to the ground. Push yourself up into a plank, then lean back into your heels and push your hips into the sky to create an inverted V. Your arms and legs should be straight. Try to press your heels toward the ground.

Mindfulness Tip:
As you hold this pose, notice sensations arising throughout your body.

Breathe.

35

Rearrange Your Room

You could call feng shui (pronounced fung shway) the ancient Chinese art of interior design. It focuses on how to style your room in a way that lets good energy or "chi" flow freely and keeps bad energy out. It's also about finding a harmony between your energy and your home's energy.

Sometimes just switching things up can go a long way toward helping you feel better.

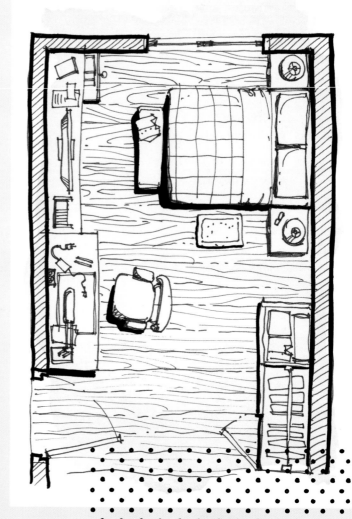

Here are some feng shui principles you can apply to your bedroom:

CHOOSE CALMING COLORS SUCH AS LIGHT BLUES, GREENS, AND LAVENDERS. EARTH TONES SUCH AS CORALS, GRAYS, AND TANS ARE ALSO PEACEFUL.

FIND DECORATIONS WITH SOFT LINES AND CURVES, NOT SHARP CORNERS.

CLEAR AWAY ALL CLUTTER, ESPECIALLY UNDER YOUR BED.

STRIVE FOR BALANCE. A SOFT BLANKET CAN COUNTER THE SHARP EDGES OF A HEADBOARD. A NIGHTSTAND ON EITHER SIDE OF YOUR BED CREATES SYMMETRY.

MOVE YOUR BED DIAGONAL FROM THE DOOR, SO YOU CAN SEE THE DOOR FROM YOUR BED, BUT YOU'RE NOT DIRECTLY IN LINE WITH IT.

HANG A PIECE OF ART THAT YOU LOVE ON THE WALL THAT FACES YOUR BED.

WHEN IT COMES TO YOUR DESK, AVOID FACING A SOLID WALL OR HAVING YOUR BACK TO THE DOOR.

GET RID OF ANY ITEM OR PHOTO THAT CAUSES YOU STRESS, THAT YOU DON'T LIKE, OR THAT BRINGS UP A BAD MEMORY.

Mindfulness Tip: As you try out different arrangements and colors in your room, really pay attention to how you feel. For example, does clearing out clutter make you feel calmer? Do pastel colors make you feel relaxed?

"INACTION BREEDS DOUBT AND FEAR. ACTION BREEDS CONFIDENCE AND COURAGE. IF YOU WANT TO CONQUER FEAR, DO NOT SIT HOME AND THINK ABOUT IT. GO OUT AND GET BUSY." – DALE CARNEGIE

Listen To Happy Music

One of the fastest ways to change your mood is by changing the tune. Studies have found that when you're looking to improve your mood, turning on some upbeat music is an easy way to get happy fast.

Luckily, being happy has always been in style! This playlist covers six decades of music that will put a smile on your face.

1960s

"You Can't Hurry Love" by The Supremes

"Here Comes the Sun" by The Beatles

"Sugar Sugar" by The Archies

"Jump in the Line (Shake, Señora)"
by Harry Belafonte

"Build Me Up Buttercup" by The Foundations

"I'm a Believer" by The Monkees

"Ain't No Mountain High Enough"
by Marvin Gaye & Tammi Terrell

"Stand by Me" by Ben E. King

1980s

"Walking on Sunshine" by Katrina and the Waves

"I Just Called (To Say I Love You)" by Stevie Wonder

"Footloose" by Kenny Loggins

"I Wanna Dance with Somebody" by Whitney Houston

"Wake Me Up Before You Go-Go" by Wham

"The Way You Make Me Feel" by Michael Jackson

"Dancing with Myself" by Billy Idol

"And She Was" by Talking Heads

"I'm Gonna Be (500 Miles)" by The Proclaimers

"Don't Worry, Be Happy" by Bobby McFerrin

2000s

"I Gotta Feeling" by Black Eyed Peas

"Beautiful Day" by U2

"All for You" by Janet Jackson

"Say Hey (I Love You)" by Michael Franti & Spearhead

"Hey Ya!" by OutKast

"Float On" by Modest Mouse

"Dog Days Are Over" by Florence + The Machine

"I Believe in a Thing Called Love" by The Darkness

"I'm Yours" by Jason Mraz

"Dynamite" by Taio Cruz

"Unwritten" by Natasha Bedingfield

1970s

"Take a Chance on Me" by ABBA

"Three Little Birds" by Bob Marley

"Mr. Blue Sky" by Electric Light Orchestra

"Don't Stop" by Fleetwood Mac

"I Can See Clearly Now" by Johnny Nash

"Imagine" by John Lennon

"Superstition" by Stevie Wonder

"One Way or Another" by Blondie

"Just What I Needed" by The Cars

1990s

"Groove Is in the Heart" by Deee-Lite

"Send Me on My Way" by Rusted Root

"MMMBop" by Hanson

"Freedom" by George Michael

"You Gotta Be" by Des'ree

"Over the Rainbow/What a Wonderful World"
by Israel Kamakawiwo'ole

"Everybody's Free (To Wear Sunscreen)"
by Baz Lurhmann

"Only Wanna Be with You" by Hootie &
the Blowfish

2010s

"Happy" by Pharrell Williams

"Uptown Funk" by Bruno Mars

"Wake Me Up" by Avicii

"Best Day of My Life" by American Authors

"Call Me Maybe" by Carly Rae Jepsen

"Get Lucky" by Daft Punk

"All About That Bass" by Meghan Trainor

"We Found Love" by Rihanna

"Burn" by Ellie Goulding

"Demons" by Imagine Dragons

"Safe and Sound" by Capital Cities

Volunteer

People who volunteer often say their stress levels are lower, they're happier, and they feel healthier. Volunteering can also help you feel more connected to others, which fights off feelings of loneliness. The results are almost instantaneous — you'll feel so great helping others that you won't want to stop.

DoSomething.org and VolunteerMatch.org are two great resources with lots of unique volunteer opportunities that can be tailored to your passions.

Here are some volunteer opportunities that are worth looking into.

HELP THE HUNGRY

Food banks are always looking for help sorting, packing, and stacking donated food items that they then give to pantries and shelters. Homeless shelters are often looking for help to serve meals throughout the year and on holidays. These are great opportunities for a group of family or friends. Find more information at **feedingamerica.org** or **homelessshelterdirectory.org**.

ASSIST A NEIGHBOR

Help mow the lawn, shovel snow, take out the trash, or rake leaves for an elderly neighbor. While daily errands can be a challenge, people of advanced age often suffer from loneliness too. Make a weekly date to spend time playing board games with an older neighbor or spend an afternoon chatting with residents at a local nursing home or senior center.

CHEER ON THE COMPETITION

Marathons and run/walks always need help passing out water and snacks and cheering on the runners. They're often raising awareness and money for a good cause. Standing on the sidelines will get your adrenaline pumping — and it might inspire you to sign up as a participant next year.

SUPPORT THE TROOPS

Deployed soldiers (the men and women who are fighting for our country overseas) love to receive notes and care packages throughout the year. Veterans, first responders, and wounded heroes also deserve thanks. Find more information at **soldiersangels.org** or **operationgratitude.com**.

GIVE BACK TO NATURE

Parks are wonderful, and it takes a lot of effort to keep them clean, groomed, and safe. The U.S. National Park Service and the U.S. Forest Service have lots of volunteer opportunities. In fact, some of their youth volunteer programs double as summer jobs. Your local park district may also organize chances to volunteer on Earth Day and other holidays. Find more information at **nps.gov** or **volunteer.gov**.

Spread Kindness

When you play a role in making other people happy, it's hard to be unhappy yourself. Write positive messages, jokes, or inspirational quotes on note cards or a pad of sticky notes. Carry them around with you, then leave one behind when the moment is right.

The notes are sure to brighten someone's day if you leave them:

ON A MIRROR IN THE BATHROOM AT SCHOOL.

IN THE CENTER OF A POPULAR BOOK OR MAGAZINE AT THE LIBRARY.

ON THE WINDSHIELD OF A CAR.

IN RANDOM LOCKERS AT SCHOOL.

ON A LUNCH TRAY.

ON A SEAT ON THE BUS.

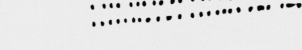

Ideas:

HOPE YOUR DAY IS GOING GREAT!

YOU'RE BEAUTIFUL!

DON'T GIVE UP!

YOU'RE ONE OF A KIND.

SMILE! IT LOOKS GOOD ON YOU.

YOU LOOK GREAT TODAY!

HAVE AN AWESOME DAY.

STAY POSITIVE!

YOU'RE STRONGER THAN YOU THINK.

TOMORROW IS ANOTHER DAY!

KEEP YOUR CHIN UP.

NEVER GIVE UP ON YOUR DREAMS.

Mindfulness Tip:
Notice how you feel when you leave one of these notes. It's a simple way to boost your mood!

IF YOU'RE COMFORTABLE WITH IT, TRY COMPLIMENTING A STRANGER IN PERSON. IT CAN BE SOMETHING SIMPLE, LIKE "WHAT A PRETTY SKIRT!" OR *"Your laugh is infectious."*

"I'VE LEARNED THAT PEOPLE WILL FORGET WHAT YOU SAID, PEOPLE WILL FORGET WHAT YOU DID, BUT PEOPLE WILL NEVER FORGET HOW YOU MADE THEM FEEL." – MAYA ANGELOU

Do You Need Help?

If you've ever thought about harming yourself or others, seek help right away. Turn to page 47 for a list of resources.

The exercises and ideas in this book offer help for short-term stress. They are not cures or treatments for more serious, long-term issues, such as chronic depression, suicidal thoughts, self-harming behavior, disordered eating, addiction, post-traumatic stress disorder, and generalized anxiety disorder.

Symptoms of more serious mental health issues, such as depression or anxiety, can include any or all of the following:

- LETHARGY AND/OR FATIGUE
- RESTLESSNESS
- FEELINGS OF GUILT
- TROUBLE SLEEPING INCLUDING OVERSLEEPING, INSOMNIA, AND RESTLESS SLEEP
- LACK OF STRENGTH OR ENERGY
- LACK OF INTEREST IN DAILY ACTIVITIES AND HOBBIES
- CHANGES IN APPETITE
- WEIGHT GAIN OR WEIGHT LOSS
- DIFFICULTY CONCENTRATING, MAKING DECISIONS, AND REMEMBERING
- LACK OF SELF-CONFIDENCE
- PERSISTENT FEELING OF SADNESS
- FEELING AS THOUGH YOUR LIFE ISN'T WORTH LIVING
- PERSISTENT PHYSICAL SYMPTOMS IN RESPONSE TO YOUR EMOTIONS (SUCH AS GETTING A HEADACHE OR STOMACHACHE AS A RESULT OF SADNESS OR ANXIETY)

- THOUGHTS OF DEATH OR SUICIDE
- MOOD SWINGS
- SOCIAL ISOLATION OR PERSISTENT FEELINGS OF LONELINESS
- CHANGE IN ENERGY LEVEL
- CHANGE IN SELF-ESTEEM
- FEELING EASILY OR OVERLY IRRITABLE
- FEELINGS OF HOPELESSNESS AND PESSIMISM
- APATHY
- EXCESSIVE CRYING
- SIGNIFICANT CHANGES IN DAILY BEHAVIOR
- LACK OF MOTIVATION
- FEELING "EMPTY"
- SLOWNESS OF ACTIVITY
- RACING THOUGHTS AND/OR EXCESSIVE WORRY
- FEELING A SENSE OF IMPENDING DANGER
- EXCESSIVE SWEATING, TREMBLING, OR SHORTNESS OF BREATH

If any of these negative feelings have been affecting you regularly for two weeks or more, you may need some extra attention. It's important to seek help as soon as possible, especially if your symptoms are affecting your relationships, your health and well-being, or your ability to fulfill your responsibilities.

How to Ask for Help

If you or a friend needs help, there are many people and resources you can turn to. A doctor, social worker, or school counselor can offer professional help. If you need help figuring out how to contact one of these people, reach out to a trusted friend, family member, or teacher.

On a day-to-day basis, friends and family members can keep you on track. Don't forget that asking for help makes you stronger, not weaker.

In addition to seeking out professional help, you can ask supportive, reliable, confident friends and family members to . . .

HELP YOU STAY POSITIVE.

LISTEN WHEN YOU NEED SOMEONE TO TALK TO.

HELP YOU CREATE AND MANAGE A SCHEDULE.

REMIND YOU THAT OTHER PEOPLE STRUGGLE TOO.

MOTIVATE YOU TO FINISH YOUR HOMEWORK ON TIME.

MAKE YOU LAUGH.

HELP YOU GET YOUR CHORES DONE.

PRAISE YOUR PROGRESS.

REMIND YOU THAT YOU WILL FEEL BETTER SOMEDAY.

WAKE YOU UP ON TIME — NO SNOOZE BUTTONS ALLOWED.

GO FOR A WALK WITH YOU.

MAKE DOCTOR APPOINTMENTS FOR YOU.

GIVE YOU PEP TALKS AND TELL YOU WHY YOU'RE GREAT.

WHO CAN HELP

National Suicide Prevention Lifeline
www.sptsusa.org
1-800-273-TALK (8255)

Substance Abuse and Mental Health Services Administration's National Helpline
www.samhsa.gov
1-800-662-HELP (4357)

National Eating Disorders Association
www.nationaleatingdisorders.org
Crisis text line: text "NEDA" to 741741
1-800-931-2237

S.A.F.E. Alternatives
www.selfinjury.com
1-800-DONT-CUT (366-8288)

Gay, Lesbian, Bisexual and Transgender National Hotline
www.glnh.org
1-888-THE-GLNH (843-4564)

The National Center for Grieving Children & Families
www.dougy.org
1-866-775-5683

National Runaway Safeline
www.1800runaway.org
1-800-RUNAWAY (786-2929)

Planned Parenthood
www.plannedparenthood.org/info-for-teens
1-800-230-PLAN (7526)

National Sexual Assault Hotline
www.rainn.org
1-800-656-HOPE (4673)

National Domestic Violence Hotline
www.thehotline.org
1-800-799-SAFE (7233)

National Alliance on Mental Illness
www.nami.org
1-800-950-6264

Read More

Beaumont, Mary Richards. *The Awesomest, Randomest Book Ever: Odd Stuff to Read & Fun Stuff to Do*. Middleton, Wis.: American Girl Publishing, 2014.

Brukner, Lauren. *The Kids' Guide to Staying Awesome and In Control: Simple Stuff to Help Children Regulate their Emotions and Senses*. Philadelphia ; London: Jessica Kingsley Publishers, 2014.

Roberts, Emily. *Express Yourself: A Teen Girl's Guide to Speaking Up and Being Who You Are*. Instant Help Books. Oakland, Calif.: New Harbinger Publications, Inc., 2015.

Internet Sites

Use FactHound to find Internet Sites related to this book.

Visit *www.facthound.com*

Just type in 9781515768203 and go.

Aubre Andrus is an award-winning children's book author with books published by Scholastic, American Girl, and more. She cherishes her time spent as the Lifestyle Editor of *American Girl* magazine where she developed crafts, recipes, and party ideas for girls. When she's not writing, Aubre loves traveling around the world, and some of her favorite places include India, Cambodia, and Japan. She currently lives in Los Angeles with her husband. You can find her website at www.aubreandrus.com.

A mindfulness practitioner for almost 40 years and a lifelong educator, Dr. Karen Bluth is faculty at University of North Carolina at Chapel Hill. Her research focuses on the roles that self-compassion and mindfulness play in promoting well-being in youth. She is author of *The Self-Compassion Workbook for Teens* (New Harbinger Publishers) and co-creator of the curriculum *Making Friends with Yourself: A Mindful Self-Compassion Program for Teens*.

KOHLER ELEMENTARY LIBRARY
KOHLER, WISCONSIN